Volcanoes

by Joelle Riley

Lerner Publications Company • Minneapolis

Photo Acknowledgments

The images in this book are used with the permission of: © Photodisc/Getty Images, pp. 1, 9, all backgrounds; AP Photo/Malut Post, Purwanto, p. 4; © Pacific Stock/SuperStock, pp. 6, 8, 17, 24; AP Photo/Steve Young, p. 7; © age fotostock/SuperStock, p. 10; AP Photo/Ted S. Warren, p. 12; © Greg Martin/SuperStock, p. 13; © Kim Westerskov/Stone/Getty Images, p. 14; © Science VU/NURP/Visuals Unlimited, p. 16; © David Matherly/Visuals Unlimited, p. 18; © J.D. Griggs/U.S. Geological Survey, p. 20; © Roger Ressmeyer/CORBIS, p. 21; AP Photo/Dolores Ochoa R., p. 22; AP Photo/Itsuo Inouye, p. 26; © Travel Ink/Gallo Images/Getty Images, p. 27. Illustration on p. 28 by © Laura Westlund/Independent Picture Service.

Front cover: © Art Wolfe/The Image Bank/Getty Images.
Back cover: © Photodisc/Getty Images.

Lerner Publications Company
A division of Lerner Publishing Group, Inc.
241 First Avenue North
Minneapolis, MN 55401 U.S.A.

Website address: www.lernerbooks.com

Words in **bold type** are explained in a glossary on page 31.

Library of Congress Cataloging-in-Publication Data

Riley, Joelle.
    Volcanoes / by Joelle Riley.
        p.   cm. — (Pull ahead books-forces of nature)
    Includes index.
    ISBN 978-0-8225-7909-0 (lib. bdg. : alk. paper)
    1. Volcanoes—Juvenile literature. I. Title.
QE521.3.R55 2008
551.21—dc22   2007024902

Manufactured in the United States of America
1 2 3 4 5 6 – JR – 13 12 11 10 09 08

Table of Contents

Mount Gamkonora in Indonesia

What Is a Volcano?

This mountain is a **volcano**. It looks different from most mountains. How is it different? Most mountains are quiet and still. But this mountain is rumbling. The volcano is **erupting**. Steam and **ash** are coming out of it. Ash is small bits of rock.

Hot, melted rock comes out of other volcanoes. The melted rock is called **lava**.

Lava is so hot that it glows bright red. Slowly, the lava cools. It hardens into solid rock.

Some volcanoes erupt slowly. Lava oozes out of these volcanoes. The lava flows across the ground. It looks like a river made of fire.

Other volcanoes erupt quickly. Lava,
hot rocks, and ash fly through the air.

Krakatoa Volcano in Indonesia

Will the Volcano Erupt?

Some volcanoes erupt for a little while. Then they stop. Other volcanoes keep erupting for years. A volcanoe that is erupting is called an **active volcano**.

Scientists use special tools to tell if a volcano will erupt.

Some volcanoes haven't erupted for a while. But scientists think they will erupt again. These volcanoes are called **dormant volcanoes**.

Some volcanoes probably will never erupt again. Scientists call them **extinct volcanoes**.

An extinct volcano in the state of Alaska

White Island in New Zealand

Where Volcanoes Are Found

Volcanoes are found in many places. Most of the world's volcanoes are found around the Pacific Ocean. This area has so many volcanoes that people call it the Ring of Fire.

Some volcanoes are hidden under the ocean. When an underwater volcano erupts, the lava hardens quickly.

Underwater view of lava rocks near the state of Hawaii

Lava rock piles up underwater. After a long time, the pile of lava reaches the water's surface. An **island** forms.

Parinacota Volcano in Chile

When Volcanoes Erupt

This volcano is dormant. Its top is covered with snow. If the volcano erupts, the snow will melt. The melted snow will mix with soil. It will become mud. Mud will flow down the volcano. Flowing mud can knock down buildings and trees. It can hurt people and animals.

Flowing lava can be dangerous too.
Hot lava can burn buildings.

Lava can bury cars. But lava flows slowly. People and animals can usually get away from it.

This family moved to safety when a volcano
erupted near their home in Ecuador.

Staying Safe

Scientists study volcanoes. They want to learn more about how volcanoes erupt. Sometimes scientists think a dormant volcano is about to erupt. They warn people who live nearby. The people can go to a safer place.

Helpful Volcanoes

Lava rock from a volcano is hard. But over many years, rain, wind, and water break it into bits. The bits of rock become soil. Soil made from lava is good for growing plants.

People left their nearby homes when this volcano erupted in Japan.

Active volcanoes are very dangerous.

But volcanoes can be helpful too.

Plants grow well in soil with bits of lava rock in it.

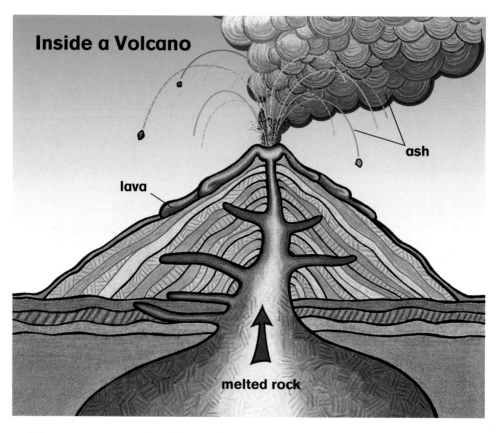

Inside a Volcano

ash

lava

melted rock

Big spaces under Earth's surface are filled with hot, melted rock. Volcanoes form above these spaces. Sometimes melted rock pushes upward through the ground. It flows out of a volcano. The volcano erupts.

Volcano Facts

- Earth has more than 500 active volcanoes. Most of them are around the Pacific Ocean.

- Most of the active volcanoes in the United States are in the states of Hawaii, Alaska, California, Oregon, and Washington.

- Crater Lake is in the state of Oregon. The lake formed when a volcano exploded and lost its top more than 6,000 years ago. Water filled in the crater.

- People who lived in Hawaii long ago believed in a goddess named Pele. The people thought that when Pele got angry, she made volcanoes erupt.

- Mauna Kea is a volcano in Hawaii. It is Earth's tallest volcano. It is more than 5 miles (8 kilometers) high when measured from its base, which is under the ocean.

- The largest volcano in our solar system is on the planet Mars. It is called Olympus Mons. This volcano is nearly three times as tall as Earth's tallest mountain.

Further Reading

Books

Dinaberg, Leslie. *Volcanoes*. Chanhassen, MN: Child's World, 2007.

Fradin, Judy, and Dennis Fradin. *Volcanoes*. Washington, DC: National Geographic, 2007.

Storad, Conrad J. *Earth's Crust*. Minneapolis: Lerner Publications Company, 2007.

Walker, Sally M. *Volcanoes*. Minneapolis: Lerner Publications Company, 2008.

Websites

Facts about Volcanoes for Kids
http://www.woodlands-junior.kent.sch.uk/Homework/mountains/volcanoes.htm
You can learn what causes volcanoes, play games, and read stories.

Kids' Door
http://volcano.und.edu/vwdocs/kids/kids.html
Learn more interesting facts about volcanoes on a fun website for kids.

Volcanoes
http://www.fema.gov/kids/volcano.htm
This site has everything you want to know about volcanoes plus games and a volcanoes quiz.

Glossary

active volcanoes: volcanoes that are erupting

ash: small bits of rock that come out of a volcano

dormant volcanoes: volcanoes that haven't erupted for a while but will probably erupt again

erupting: giving off steam, bits of rock, or melted rock

extinct volcanoes: volcanoes that scientists think will never erupt again

island: a piece of land that is surrounded by water

lava: hot, melted rock that comes out of a volcano

volcano: an opening in the ground out of which steam, bits of rock, or melted rock comes

Index